123
SESAME STREET®

Go Green with Sesame Street

BE WATER-WISE, SUPER GROVER!

Lerner Publications ◆ Minneapolis

Cooperating and sharing are an important part of *Sesame Street*—and of taking care of our planet. We all share Earth, so it's up to all of us to take care of it together. The *Go Green with Sesame Street*® books cover everything from appreciating Earth's beauty, to conserving its resources, to helping keep it clean, and more. And the familiar, furry friends from *Sesame Street* offer young readers some easy ways to help protect their planet.

Sincerely,

The Editors at Sesame Workshop

The text of this book is printed on paper that is made with 30 percent recycled postconsumer waste fibers.

Table of Contents

A Water Hero   **4**

We Use Water Every Day   **6**

Water Worries   **12**

Save Water   **18**

Earth Day Every Day   28
Recycled Rain   30
Glossary   31
Index   32

A Water Hero

What a puzzle! I hear the water running, but I see no one at the sink. I, Super Grover, must save the water!

We Use Water Every Day

People need fresh water to drink. Fresh water comes from rivers and lakes. Most of Earth's water is in oceans. But ocean water is salty.

We cannot drink salt water—it makes us even *thirstier*. Can we turn salt water into fresh water, Zoe?

We can, Super Grover— but it takes a *lot* of time, money, and energy.

Animals need fresh water to drink too.

Plants need water to grow. Plants take in water through their roots.

Wow, water will help that plant grow!

People use water for cleaning. We wash dishes, cars, and clothes—and ourselves! We also use water to have fun.

Water Worries

We need to make sure there's enough fresh water for everyone on Earth.

We all share the same planet!

Aww, me love to share!

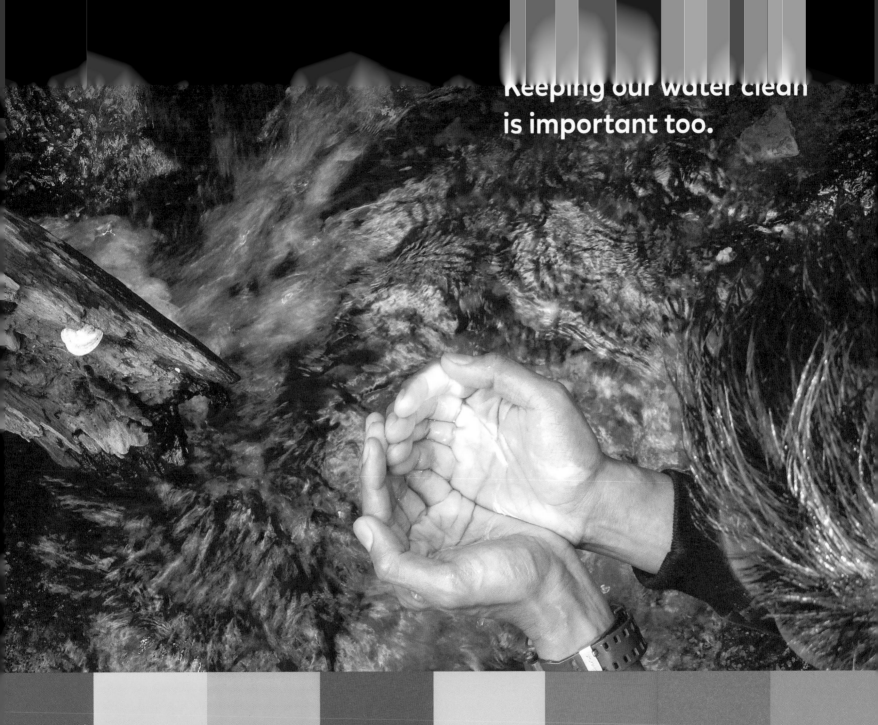

Keeping our water clean
is important too.

Sometimes people flush the wrong things down the drain.

Don't flush cotton swabs or wipes! They make the water dirty.

Put trash where it belongs—with me!

Things like cotton balls or floss can end up in water nearby.

Litter, or trash, pollutes water. That's bad for people and animals.

Many people work hard to clean Earth's water. People also try to use less.

You can help protect water too. Being a water hero is a super job!

Save Water

Flush only toilet paper down the drain.

Elmo wants to flush the *right* things!

Make sure to throw trash in the right container. You can recycle paper, plastic, and more.

When you brush your teeth, use only the water you need. Use just a little water to wash your hands.

21

In a bath, use only enough water to cover your legs. Try to keep your showers short.

It takes a lot of water to make paper. If you draw on both sides, you use less.

Help keep the water where you live clean. Use only the water you need. Can you think of more ways to save water?

Earth Day Every Day

Earth Day is on April 22. People celebrate Earth in different ways. One way is to clean up beaches or rivers.

Saving water makes every day Earth Day!

Recycled Rain

Use rain in a new way!

1. Ask an adult for some empty plastic containers.

2. Decorate the containers.

3. Put the containers outside to catch rain.

4. Use your recycled rain to water indoor plants!

Glossary

container: something that holds something else

litter: trash people throw on the ground or in water

pollutes: makes dirty

protect: to keep from danger or harm

Index

fresh water, 6–7, 8, 12

lakes, 6

oceans, 6

plants, 9

rivers, 6

salt water, 7

Photo Acknowledgments

Additional image credits: vectorau/Shutterstock.com, throughout (background); LisaValder/Getty Images, p. 5; Sasiistock/Getty Images, p. 6; Betty4240/Getty Images, p. 8; Blend Images - JGI/Jamie Grill/Getty Images, p. 10; Axel Bernstorff/Getty Images, p. 11; Putra Kurniawan/EyeEm/Getty Images, p. 13; Herianus Herianus/EyeEm/Getty Images, p. 15; Africa Studio/Shutterstock.com, p. 16; Rawpixel.com/Shutterstock.com, p. 19; Hero Images/Getty Images, pp. 20, 28; Hung Chung Chih/Shutterstock.com, p. 22; Klaus Vedfelt/Getty Images, p. 24; Caiaimage/Trevor Adeiline/Getty Images, p. 26; Monkey Business Images/Shutterstock.com, p. 29; Chayapat Kaewnarin/Shutterstock.com, p. 30.

Cover: Background material/Shutterstock.com (background), Happiest Sima/Shutterstock.com (rain).

Lerner Publications Company
An imprint of Lerner Publishing Group, Inc.
241 First Avenue North
Minneapolis, MN 55401 USA

For reading levels and more information, look up this title at www.lernerbooks.com.

Main body text set in Mikado. Typeface provided by HVD.

Library of Congress Cataloging-in-Publication Data

Names: Boothroyd, Jennifer, 1972- author.
Title: Be water-wise, super Grover! / Jennifer Boothroyd.
Description: Minneapolis : Lerner Publications, [2020] | Series: Go green with Sesame Street | Includes index.
Identifiers: LCCN 2019013422 (print) | LCCN 2019018588 (ebook) | ISBN 9781541572591 (library binding : alk. paper) | ISBN 9781541583146 (eb pdf)
Subjects: LCSH: Water conservation—Juvenile literature. | Earth Day—Juvenile literature. | Grover (Fictitious character : Henson)—Juvenile literature.
Classification: LCC TD388 .B66 2020 (print) | LCC TD388 (ebook) | DDC 333.91/16—dc23

LC record available at https://lccn.loc.gov/2019013422
LC ebook record available at https://lccn.loc.gov/2019018588

Manufactured in the United States of America
1-46526-47571-8/6/2019